THE SACRED WORDS

The Sacred Words

Cover design by the author
www.MelanieDTheAuthor.com

Mauramore Press
ISBN: 979-8-234-05375-6 (paperback)
Printed in the United States of America

First Edition

THE
Sacred Words

POEMS ON FAITH, LOVE AND CONSEQUENCE

by

MELANIE D. WEST

For you,
who aim to love well,
listen intently,
and speak gently,

and for those whose stories are held within these pages:
some lived, some witnessed, some shared with me by others.

AUTHOR'S NOTE

Have you ever sung along to a song you loved, only to stop and wonder, *Wait, what did they just say? What am I singing?*

Have you ever noticed how people, places and things respond to the words you speak, or how the words spoken to you most often make you feel?

This book was born from a simple question:

What are we really saying, and how can we use our words for good?

We live in a world where language is often handled carelessly, especially the words we reserve for love. This collection is an invitation to slow down, to treat speech as sacred, and to consider the weight of what we say, what we withhold, and what is spoken in our hearing.

The Sacred Words is not a manual on love, nor a sermon. It is a meditation on what it means to speak with care, walk with integrity, and live what we declare. Rooted in the wisdom of 1 Corinthians 13 and echoing the prayer of Psalm 19:14, these poems explore love as action, restraint, courage, and covenant.

If these pages ask anything of the reader, it is this:

Say less.
Mean more.
Live it.

These poems were written over the years,
each piece thoughtfully gathered for this collection.
Where noted, the year reflects the original time of writing;
some pieces were previously shared online,
while others, both old and new,
are being published here
for the first time.

CONTENTS

I. THE WORDS WE MEAN 1
The Sacred Words 2
Only if I Can Live It 4
Sincere Heart 5
Before I Say It 6
I Choose You 7
Altars 8
Virtue of Becoming 9
King Energy 11
Home 13
Just Us 14
I Love Your Music 15
As Long As I Love 16
No You Without Her 17
Inheritance 18
Covered in Prayer 19
Grateful 21
Misunderstood 22
Before I Learned the Language 24
Hallowed 25
Lifelines 26
A Measure of Love 27
What Love Says Daily 28
What a Privilege 29

II. THE WORDS WE WITHHOLD 31
Almost 32
Silent Sentiment 33
Say It While You Can 34
Small Talk 36
Say Their Names 37
The Last Page 38
When Words Fail 39
Love Untranslated 40
The Perfect Sentence 41
First Love 42
Secret Place 43
Nothing Missing 44
Generations 45
Later 47

III. THE WORDS THAT WOUND 49
You Didn't Mean It That Way 50
Sugar and Spice 51
Once It Leaves 52
Fox Trot 53
Subliminals 54
Unexpected 55
Silent Witness 56
In God's Name 57
Bully 60
The Audacity of Freedom 61
You've Met Her Before 62
Empty 65
What You Answer To 67
Imprint 69
Still Unlearning 70

IV. THE WORDS THAT HEAL 71
Your Voice Matters 72
Love Lifted Me 73
Resurrection 74
The Grudge 75
I Forgive You 76
Say It Again, Slower 78
Learning a Softer Language 79
Honey 80
The Church Alive 81
The Right Mix 82

Sanctuary *83*
Love Has Always Been Our Power *84*
What Grace Sounds Like *86*
When The World Stood Still *87*
Job's Song *89*
Reclaimed Words *90*
Stones or Seeds *92*
What the Wind Brings Back *95*
The Seed *96*
Celeb-rated *97*
Gatekeeper *99*

V. THE WORDS GOD SPEAKS 101
Before You Spoke *102*
I'm Here *103*
I Asked God a Question *104*
Rainbow On My Door *105*
Called By Name *106*
My View *108*
I Hear Your Prayers *110*
In The Stillness *111*
Still Speaking *112*
Listen *113*
Honey From The Rock *115*
Heaven's Vocabulary *116*
Your Times Are In My Hands *117*
Return To Me *118*
The Word Became Flesh *119*
It Is Written *121*
GOD IS LOVE *124*

VI. AFTERLIGHT 125
Fireflies *126*
They That Wait *127*
They Shall Not Want *129*
Peace from Sunrise to Sonrise *131*
Song in the Night *133*
The Sermon of Morning *135*
Sermon of Submission *136*
The Pages of You *137*
What Remains *138*
Candlelight *139*
Inseparable *141*

SECTION I.
THE WORDS WE MEAN

Words spoken with care, love, and intention.

The Sacred Words

"I love you" ain't just breath,
not just sound that floats on air.
It bears the weight of covenant.
It's heart-sown, spirit-born, rare.

It's patience wrapped in promise,
kindness stitched with truth,
a genuine expression
reinforced by proof.

It doesn't brag, doesn't bruise,
doesn't lean toward pride.
To shine, it never throws shade
on someone else's light.

"I love you" is sacred,
because love itself is holy.
Never in haste or loosely;
spoken truly, only.

Love bears what it must,
believes when roads grow bleak,
shines in the darkest night,
stays strong when you feel weak.

Love hopes past the breaking point,
endures stormy weather,
through all that comes, unbroken still,
holding fast forever.

When you say the sacred words,
you echo heaven's tone,
the language that never fails,
and never will grow old.

It's God's own heart
revealed and shared,
an earnest declaration
that shows how much you care.

So let those words be
rare enough to honor,
true enough to keep,
strong enough to lift,
soft enough to weep,

and pure enough to mirror
the One that spoke them first,
the same God that still speaks now
and embodies every word…

God is Love.

Only If I Can Live It

I won't say it lightly.
I've learned words
can bruise when they're thrown,
or sown falsely.

"I love you"
is an anchor between hearts,
not a passing phrase.

It means I stay
when staying costs me.
It means I listen
without rehearsing my escape.

If I say it,
I will mean tomorrow
as much as today.

Because love spoken
without commitment
is only noise.

Sincere Heart

I said it
not to bind,
not to bargain,
not to keep.

I said it
because it is true.

Because my heart spoke
what it could not hold back,
what was felt with sincerity.

Love is given,
not pursued.
What you do with that
is up to you.

Before I Say It

I aim to weigh my words
before they leave my mouth,
holding them against my chest
like fragile glass.

If they break,
they cut both ways.

So I'll assert my power,
walking heavy at times,
but speaking gently…
raising my voice only to be heard,
not to harm.

I'll say it with my chest,
knowing love doesn't need
many decibels or syllables.

I'll show it with my life,
because sometimes there are no words.

I Choose You

There are no perfect words,
nor a perfect life hereafter.

There are days when love is easy,
days of joy and laughter.

There is sorrow that comes knocking,
days when hearts are tossed by feeling.

Days of plenty and of little,
days of health and days of healing.

But this is what we're choosing,
however days are leaning.

The ring is just a token
'til faithfulness gives it meaning.

What we mean today
is simple enough to say,
but deep enough to spend a lifetime proving:

I choose you.
Again and again.

Altars

No aisle.
No witnesses.
No rings catching light.

Just two hearts
deciding to live the truth
out loud.

Love is what you choose,
and do consistently,
after the moment passes
and no one is watching.

Virtue of Becoming

I rise while the house is still quiet,
sometimes while it is still night,
whisper my prayers, then listen
for the Help each moment demands.

I set my hands to what this day requires;
some days it is strength,
some days, softness,
and most days,
learning both without apology.

I am not the perfect woman written in gold,
but the one still unfolding.

I will do good
not only in grand gestures,
but in subtler ways:
meals made carefully,
words of wisdom said prayerfully,
and silence, when peace matters more than being right.

My worth is not in the noise I make,
but in the balance I create
when life leans a little heavy.

I will laugh and spread joy where I can,
and when I cannot,
I will still be there with love in my hands
and faith in my spine.

I will consider and tend the field
of the lives entrusted to me,
pulling weeds of resentment
before they grow roots,
planting kindness where fatigue tries to stew.

Strength will not always look like stone.
Sometimes it will look like gentleness
when I am tired of being strong.

And I will not pretend I never falter.

But I will always rise again,
gathering and storing,
receiving and pouring,
unwrapping my gifts in the marketplace,
and showing up for the ones I love.

So let it be said of me,
that I was faithful in becoming,
a woman who feared God
and learned to trust Him
with her imperfect, honest life.

And if I am a jewel in His crown,
then let me be one
still being shaped in grace
and ever putting a smile
on His face.

King Energy

I do not rise to be seen,
I rise to be a reflection of the King.

Before the world asks anything of me,
I lay my thoughts before God
and ask for a clean heart
before a strong hand.

I now understand that power without humility
is only noise wearing confidence,
so I try to walk slower than my pride
and speak softer than my certainty.

Besides, I am not perfect,
but I am accountable.
I do not claim mastery
over what I won't live out in private.

I work with my hands and my mind,
building, providing, pressing forward.
I do not wait for life to hand me purpose,
I deploy it.

I bring back what is needed,
not just for myself,
but for those who depend on my shelter.

I honor the women in my life,
and those who shaped me,
through words and consistency,
loyalty and esteem.

I lead, but I do not lord.
I protect, but I do not possess.
I build, but I do not boast.

And when I fail,
I do not hide behind ego
or excuse myself from growth.
I return to God, and take note.

I have learned that real strength
does not announce itself.
It shows up,
it stays,
it serves.

So I walk as a man still being refined,
imperfect and present;
humble and aligned;
not a king above others,
but a man accountable to God
for how I treat each soul in my path.

And if I am to be called strong,
let it be because I learned
to walk in faith and temperance
and lead with love.

Home (2011)

Your eyes are just one of the reasons I love you.
How they light up when I catch a glimpse
and smile back at me.

How they look deep into mine
and transfer the warmth of your heart.

And all I find, there,
is absolute joy and contentment,
sincere respect, trust, and devotion
beneath those eyes, crystallized with emotion.

They cease to roam
because they know the search is over,
and they've found a place to call home.

Just Us

I don't say it
to impress the room.

I say it
when it's just us,
no fuss, no glitz,
when your guard is down,
when your name feels safe
on my lips.

"I love you"
means I notice
how you wake from sleep,
the way your eyes meet mine first thing,
your small morning rituals,
daily rhythms and evening unwinds,
how you make time
for God, for me.

I see you.

Your smile when you're feeling sunny,
how you sometimes laugh when you want to cry,
how you get quiet
when the day has been rough,
yet still push through
when I need your gentle touch.

It means
I tend to your garden,
choosing you
in the long hours,
not just the beautiful ones,
and giving you your flowers
before the day is done.

I Love Your Music

I love your music:
the drumming of your pulse,
sending morse code to mine;

the rhythm of your lashes,
flashing those beautiful lamps
between soft winds.

The lift and lull of your tone,
like a metronome;
even your silences keep time.

The soft percussion of your laughter,
trailing after your sunshine smile;
your feet colliding with gravity,
making your whole being
poetry in motion,

a cadence and stride that glide
across the atmosphere
with a swag unmistakable.

I can hear your thoughts form
milliseconds before your mouth
forms the words,
'cause I've learned your rhythm
and I know you well.

I love your music.

As Long As I Love

You came into my life
like a prayer I once prayed
that never forgot where to find me.

A breath of fresh air,
like the first sign of spring after a long winter.

Truth says love transcends the grave.
Still, as long as I live, I'll love you.
And as long as I love, I'm living.
Life is sweeter, and breathing feels easier
because of you.

No You Without Her

A mother's love
is God's imprint on a heart
and God's echo in a house:
soft in presence, strong in covering,
secure when life is not.

Simple moments with her
are like a slice of heaven,
her love among the first signs
God is good.

Through her you entered the world,
passed from darkness into light,
from a seed to life.

And having her in your life
just makes sense...
there is no you without her,
you wouldn't have made it through without her,
you wouldn't know your roots without her
or the places she lives in you without her.

She's one of one,
and no one could ever take her place.

Inheritance

Before your first cry breaks the silence,
before your feet touch the ground,
I place these words
as an arch over your life,
to cover and surround.

May you know you
before the world tries to claim you.
May truth steady you
when lies come to frame you.

May your strength be tempered with mercy,
and love overwhelm you with grace.
May peace settle and keep you
when fear stares you in the face.

May you stand when the road dips
or grows costly.
And when the night presses in,
you keep walking.

And if ever you forget
what was spoken over you,
may it rise again and imbue,

as choices that steer you right,
and character that shines a light,
and as the wind you carry others on
when they can't quite carry themselves.

This is what you come from,
what you must carry on.
May these words resound,
be remembered and lived,
long after my voice is gone.

Covered In Prayer

I remember prayers heard from the other room,
and kneeling together in the living room,
in doorways before going to school;
prayers beyond church were the rule.

I remember oily foreheads
and dabs throughout the house,
hands laid and placed over me, covering my life.

There were prayers in the car
on busy streets and highways,
keeping accidents and incidents held at bay;
prayers to quell road rage and anger,
holding back hurt, harm, and danger.

Grace wasn't just common, it was every day.
We knew to thank God before we ate,
knowing by His hands we all were fed,
and thanking Him for our daily bread.
We'd bless the hands that prepared our meal
and ask that it strengthen, nourish and build.
And even for those without food to eat,
we'd ask that God would supply their need.

And yes, before the close of day,
just as we were taught to say,
we'd ask to be forgiven, that our wrongs be erased
and we learned to forgive others with that same grace.

Before we'd lay ourselves to sleep
we'd pray the Lord our souls to keep.
And should no one tuck us in once there,
we knew we were already covered in prayer.

And the beauty is,
prayers don't have expiration dates.
Like incense, they rise to the heavenly place.

And it's such a comfort to know...
that every petition, travail and prayer,
spoken then and even there,
is bearing fruit in my life today
and it reminds me now to always pray.

Grateful

For every hand that held mine,
for every word that lifted me,
for every heart that stayed kind,
for every soul that let me be,
thank you.

For the faith you kept when I couldn't see it,
for the push beyond what's behind
for the strength, life, and peace you gave
without taking from mine.

Who I am,
how I give,
what I do
traces back to you.

Thank you.

Misunderstood

I meant care,
but it felt like restriction.

I meant concern,
but it sounded like doubt.

I meant honesty,
but it landed like harm.

I meant I was tired,
that I needed to recharge,
but it came across as distance.

I meant growth,
a desire for us to go higher,
but it was heard as dissatisfaction.

I meant caution,
but it was taken as fear.

I meant wait,
but it drew conclusions to never.

Human words are clumsy
when they leave the heart.
They don't always arrive
the way they were sent.

Sometimes love
speaks fluently inside
and stumbles out loud.

So if you misunderstood me,
if I got it wrong or I wasn't clear,
know this:

my intention was never pain,
never confusion,
never walls,
never anything but truth,
in love.

That's all.

Before I Learned the Language

Ode to God

Before I learned
how to say it to anyone else,
You spoke it over me.

You said it
with breath in my lungs,
with mercy that waited,
with patience that stayed.

You said it
with a life of sacrifice,
with love that paid the price
even when it cost everything.

You said it
in morning light
that finds me anew,
in seasons that sustain me,
in beauty that remains, reminding me
I am not forgotten.

You said it
through hands that reach for me,
through friends and family,
through gifts You placed inside me
before I knew what to call them.

You said it
with abundant life and joy overflowing,
knowing You and being known by You,
with a promise stronger than death,
with presence that never left.

So when I speak love now,
I echo Your tone,
hoping my life sounds like gratitude.

Hallowed

I speak Your name carefully,
as one whose lips know holy fire.
Not because You are fragile,
but because I am the pyre.

You are not the kind of God
Who fits inside the box
of human explanation
or dwells in structures made by hands,
as if You're man's creation.

You are the One before Whom
fire becomes a servant,
mountains fall into the sea,
the sun and moon hold their orbit,
and all creation bends its knee.

Nothing approaches You as equal.
Nothing counsels You or restrains.
Yet everything answers to You,
You're the King of kings Who reigns.

So I lower myself,
not out of reverent fear alone,
but because truth has weight,
and Your presence makes it known.

You are not merely loved, You are revered.
You are not merely honored, You are enthroned.
Any crown placed on another
falls beneath Your glory shone.

In Your presence, I remember
the privilege it is to enter,
and nothing, nor I, before Your majesty
could ever be the center.
Hallowed be Your name.

Lifelines

Love is life is love,
oxygen to the soul,
and it keeps coming back,
like blood pumping through veins,
putting down roots beneath the skin...
this is how life begins,
and what lives on after we're gone.

A Measure of Love

To borrow Your words,
I hope I have been patient enough
to give You time to act
when I didn't feel like waiting,
kind enough to speak to You
with the reverence You deserve.

I hope I have loved as You love,
not boastful, envious or proud,
but as You would;
with gentleness, selflessness, hope and will
to always seek what is good.

I hope You see the joy I find in Your truth,
the burden I carry to forgive,
as You have forgiven me, too,
how I celebrate life and beauty in others
because they remind me of You,
and how I seek to honor the sacred
in all You've created and do.

I hope what I do for You
and others makes a mark,
that You see Your heart
reflected in mine.

And for all the ways You love,
guide and sustain me, thank You.
May it spill onto others in kind.

Through every moment of doubt,
every rush and every pause,
I have tried to remember You through it all.

I just want You to know:
I love You.

What Love Says Daily

Not all love speaks in vows or grand display,
nor enters rooms with trumpets or with flame;
More often it is found in common day,
in small repeated acts without acclaim.

It sounds like checking if you made it home
or saving you the last and better part;
it stays when joy has somewhere else to roam
and keeps a lighted window in the heart.

It shows itself when life is less than fair,
when patience must outlast a heavy day;
when someone comes to show you that they care
and helps you bear what words cannot allay.

Some seek the glow of sunrise, then turn when skies grow rough;
the quiet tongue of faithfulness is love.

What a Privilege

What a privilege it is
to come before the King,
and call Him friend.

I say King because He is sovereign.
I say friend because He stays.

He leans in closely as I pray,
at full attention, listening,
as if nothing else matters
but what's weighing on my heart.

This is the place
where gratitude starts,
where His daily bread is meat,
where I ask for help without pretense,
where I lay it all at His feet.

Where forgiveness moves both ways,
where repentance has no script;
no rehearsed excuses,
just a heart undone, stripped,
and yet still welcomed.

It's the place where I bring the whole truth:
the praise, the ache, the questions,
the words that matter most,
and the speechless moments I need direction.

Here, I speak names not my own:
loved ones, strangers, neighbors, foes,
those who cannot find the words,
those whose strength is running low.

Standing in the gap, I intercede,
and He lifts my burden, meets my need.

In this place, neither volume
nor performance, nor vocabulary matters.
It's proximity, humility,
and bold, unhindered access.
Not because I deserve,
but because I'm invited.
And what a delight it is.

This is not a place
of vain repetition
or an occasion for manipulation,
for bending heaven toward my wants
or taking matters into my hands.
Not a list of demands
dressed in holy language.

It is alignment.
A listening as much as a speaking.
A refinement, a yielding,
until my will weakens
and His settles in place,
until ambition quiets
and trust is embraced.

This is the place I go, in private,
my posture fitting my need.
Standing, sitting, kneeling, or bowed,
'til there He meets me.

The place I come empty and leave filled.
The place I come questioning and leave heard.
The place I come hurting and leave consoled.

Where I remember
I was never meant to carry
everything alone.

SECTION II.

THE WORDS WE WITHHOLD

Silences held and truths left unsaid.

Almost

There are moments
when closeness makes silence
feel intentional.

Names are easy to say,
but certain words that follow
carry weight.

They press against the chest,
held hostage by fear
or uncertainty,
and remain unsaid.

Honesty is rehearsed
in solitary rooms,
spoken perfectly
to empty space.

There are times
an invitation leans in,
subtle and unannounced,
and is misread.

This is where courage hesitates.
Where confession waits
for permission
it never needed.

No lie is told.
The truth just isn't
told in time.

Silent Sentiment

It lives behind the teeth,
pressed against the tongue,
heavy with consequence.

It is tasted
in shared laughter,
in lingering moments,
in early goodbyes.

We tell ourselves
silence is maturity,
that restraint is wisdom,
that waiting is love,
and it's true.

But the soul remembers
what the heart refuses.

The words echo
in places once shared,
fully formed,
finally brave,
but no longer timely.

Some words don't disappear.
They float on the wind,
landing where hearts are open
and ears are ready.

Say It While You Can

If you notice something good,
say it.

If someone makes the room lighter
just by being in it,
convey it.

If a kindness stays with you
longer than the moment,
declare it.

If you hear something
powerful or inspiring,
share it.

Words are not small things.
They tend to settle deep.
They become mirrors,
medicine, or courage
we didn't know
we were allowed to keep.

When you see
something great in someone,
acknowledgment is key.

And when you love someone,
tell them.
No theatrics,
just honesty.

You never know
what weight or doubt you might lift,
what small miracle your voice could spark,
what long night you might ease,
how deeply your words could touch a heart.

And when you don't say it,
consider this too:
what affirmation failed,
what joy was delayed,
what good never reached the world
because it stayed inside you.

Silence speaks volumes.
So does speech.

Let your words flow,
like life-giving rivers to the soul.
Say it while you can.

Small Talk

We ended that day
like any other one.
No warning bell,
no setting sun.
No weight in the air
or signal sent
to tell us this was it.

There were words
I thought I'd say someday,
forgiveness kept
and tucked away,
love folded neat
inside my chest,
and there it'd rest
while moments decayed.

Nothing cruel was said at all,
nothing grand, our topic.
Just ordinary sentences
that now feel microscopic.
What a call…
small talk never felt so small.

If I'd known time was closing in,
I'd have different words to say,
would've chosen soft but harder things,
not comfort's masquerade.

Some words grow heavier after silence.
They wait where memories lie,
an ache to be near,
asking to be said
to one who can no longer hear.

Say Their Names

When asked for stillness,
even the clock bowed its head,
as we remembered.
In that brief unwritten space,
their names filled everything.

The Last Page

A life reduced to a letter
that can't be answered,
as if needing to have
the last word
in those last moments.
A final attempt
to be heard.

Silence reads the rest.

When Words Fail

Some pain
cannot be spoken to.

Love answers anyway
by staying.

Love Untranslated

At times, survival
disguises itself as strength.

In some homes,
love isn't absent,
just untranslated.
Praise stays implied.
Affection is practical,
rarely spoken out loud.

Some learn young
how to take up less space,
how to raise voices
without being heard,
how to pretend
they don't need
what they need most.

Rarely, if ever,
are such words spoken:
"I see you."
"You matter."
"I'm proud of you."
Not without conditions.

So growth happens
like a rose through concrete.
Hunger is carried around
like a child with no name,
mistaken for independence.

Some words,
when withheld long enough,
turn into questions
we spend adulthood answering.

The Perfect Sentence

There are moments
that outgrow language
and leave you breathless.
Love is the sentence...
and the searching heart
sighs relief.

First Love

Beating heart to heart,
seeing eye to eye,
we met on one wavelength,
spoke the same language,
laughed and found joy in simple things,
sat in easy silences.

Then the quiet shifted,
laughter stilled,
harmony became tug-of-war
for one will over the other,
and conversation ceased.

Peace was disrupted…
Momentary detours and distractions
became my daily bread,
but my soul was not being fed.

It seemed a gulf was between us,
and I had no bridge to cross.

If only His will had stayed my center,
His peace my grounding,
that still, small voice
the one I listened for...

Then I heard there was a Mediator,
One to bridge the gap,
Who daily intercedes for me
to bring us back in tune…

And once again,
He walks with me, talks with me,
reminds me I am His own.
Even though I had drifted,
His love still leads me home.

Secret Place (2010)

There is a place so deep,
safety lives there.
Joy walks hand in hand with peace,
ripples of love everywhere.

From heart to heart, words interchange,
unspoken, but clear.
Intimacy knows no range,
total extinction of fear.

Nearer, my God, to Thee,
engulfed within Your glory.
I never want to leave
this blissful refuge for me.

Inner sanctum so serene,
taste of the sweet by and by.
Like I walked into a dream,
secret place of the Most High.

Nothing Missing

(A Lesson in Grace)

Not every absence
defines a person.

Some learn to turn inward,
to gather themselves
and build anyway.

They become their own witness,
their own affirmation.
They speak life
where none was spoken.

Divine threads woven
into their DNA,
giving them
a little more material to work with.

A hidden "Blessed" on their chest,
and an invisible cape
only they could feel.
They became their own kind of hero.

What they thought wasn't given
did not end them.
It led them to the Source
from Whom it flows,
and, like a river, made room for others.

They learned the language
by becoming fluent in grace,
saying aloud what they once
needed to hear,
and giving it
before the moment fades.

Generations

Mothers, tell your daughters.
Fathers, tell your sons.
Elders, teach the babies.
Train 'em while they're young.

Before the noise instructs them
in what matters or what pays,
before wisdom's brushed aside
by the rush of passing days.

The generals are fading,
the hours grow more late.
Those who bore the weight of battles,
built the roads, and set the stakes.

Some are stepping back in silence,
some are taking final rest,
and history is leaving us
while many still draw breath.

But those who still are standing
have so much left to give.
This is not the epilogue,
their voice is needed still.

Be what you needed younger.
Be patient. Be awake.
Use every tool you gathered,
every lesson, every ache.

Use your platforms, your experience,
your knowledge, your degrees,
your failures and your victories,
your stories, your receipts.

The pace of time has quickened,
the world may move too fast.
It may seem your voice expired,
as a version of the past.

Don't surrender truth to trends
or let the moment lead.
What was learned and earned
through faith and trials
is surely what they need.

Fathers, tell your daughters.
Mothers, tell your sons.
Elders, teach the younger.
What you carry must be passed on.

So speak, share from voices past.
Now.

Don't assume they know what's true.
Your voice must cross generations
or risk becoming lost too soon.

Later

There is a word
people save for later,
as if time were faithful,
as if life were safer.

Not now.
After I'm ready.
After this season.
After tomorrow
learns to wait and reason.

Grace is offered plainly,
without disguise or plea.
Yet we stall in the doorway,
part habit, part disbelief.

Some assume
the chance won't pass
to choose mercy,
to say yes,
to call His name
at the last
tick of the clock.

Tick-tock.
TikTok.
Faith feeds keep flooding,
their face still ain't in the Book.
IG preachers urging
them to take a look,
yet they keep scrolling.

Some carry the truth quietly,
meaning to share it
when the timing feels right,
when courage feels fuller,

when rejection feels light.

All right...
But eternity
doesn't run on intention.

There are names
we meant to mention,
souls we meant to tell,
love we meant to speak
before that last farewell.

The cost is not always visible,
but it's certainly real.
What is withheld here
echoes there,
beyond what we feel.

Now is not cruel.
Now is kind.
Now is the moment
grace stands closest in time.

Say the name.
Spread the love.
Share the light.
Choose,
while choice still stands in sight.

Some doors close quietly,
so do it today
because later
just might be too late.

SECTION III.
THE WORDS THAT WOUND

Words that hurt and leave their mark.

You Didn’t Mean It That Way

You didn’t raise your voice.
You tell yourself that's what matters.

You spoke calmly, even slowly,
as if tone alone decides damage.

Dismissal called itself honesty.
Control wore the face of care.
Disrespect hid behind humor.

“I didn’t mean it that way.”

But words don’t require reason
to leave bruises.

They settle.
They replay.
They rewrite the room
long after the speaker leaves.

And soon,
people learn to edit themselves
around certain language,
to shrink before speaking,
to pre-apologize for needing,
to smile and sugarcoat words
so they land safely.

Often without knowing it,
someone is being taught
to doubt their own voice.

But of course,
love that requires silence
or falsehood
isn’t really love at all.

Sugar and Spice

Some of our most pointed lessons come
from those with fiery boldness
and a silver tongue.

The audacity of one
whose knife was in our back
to caress the wound
with kitchen remedies and smack:

salt in the cut,
measured carefully,
seasoned with tact,
served as "healing."

They speak in cures
and offer comfort,
while pouring in vinegar.

Sugar, mixed with spice,
ain't always so nice,
no matter who serves it,
but we're learning.

Beware.

Once It Leaves

It started as a sentence,
something someone said they saw.
Just ink on paper, torn apart,
swept by the wind and gone.

Each piece went where it wanted,
no map, no way to steer.
Some landed close, some far away,
exchanged from mouth to ear.

No one could gather all of it,
no hands were quick enough.
What left as one became too much,
by distance, time, and touch.

It learned new shapes in passing mouths,
grew bolder as it spread.
What wasn't clear was filled right in,
what shifted stayed unsaid.

Online, it moved without a face,
was quickly read and shown.
Just fragments shared from screen to screen,
each one more sure than known.

Somewhere in all that scattered air,
a life was being told.
Not as it was, but as it spun,
reframed and passed along.

That's the thing about what we say:
once it leaves, it learns to move.
And what it then becomes out there
is never up to you.

Fox Trot

To ask for a heart
like it is something holy,
then handle it
like it is nothing rare.

To speak words
like notes from a symphony,
then burn them down
with half notes, day by day.

To love newness,
but not the weight that follows,
to kindle warmth
but barely tend so it grows cold,
though seeming like the heart
of one who's true,
is just the dance of
foxes trotting through.

Subliminals

They never say your name.
That's the craft of it.
Just a post at noon,
slick caption drafted.
Scripture used like smoke,
a joke with one eye open.
Point well taken, nothing spoken.
A pause in the group chat,
you know who that was pointed at.
A side-eye glance and energy dips,
a smile that dies upon the lips.

Nothing said outright,
yet it has bite.
No direct shot,
but you know who got got.

Rooms turn hot or cold
without being told.
Crowds get swayed
to blame who was shaded.
Lies get fully dressed
as concern expressed.
Rumors get sent
as hints of "discernment."
Suspicion gets aimed
for target practice.
Without facts or lived experience,
just clouded inference.

And even though no one spells it out,
it is felt out loud.
And though no one says the words,
everything is heard.

Unexpected

We imagine words before they arrive.
How they'll sound
and the way we'll feel
when we hear them.
Anticipating only certainty,
comfort, and agreement.

Then the answer comes,
different than expected,
and everything shifts.

The surprise feels like cruelty,
and the right to choose differently
strikes like a stone,
when we thought
our hearts would leap instead.

Apparently, destiny had other plans.

Silent Witness

You remember the moment.

The words thrown.
The shift in the atmosphere.
The air at a standstill.

Others heard it, saw it.
You know they did.
Clocked and recorded.

Eyes lowered.
Throats cleared.
But nothing said they had your back.

Your name hung there,
waiting for backup,
a break in the heat.

But silence chose a side.
Defense took a backseat.

The bruise wasn't only
what was said.
It was who stayed quiet,
who stood still
as it transpired.

Afterward,
the air feigned its ease.

But the moment kept its grip,
and you learned to breathe
through it.

In God's Name

It didn't sound
or seem cruel
at first.

It felt careful.
Measured.
Certain.

It came cloaked in scripture,
laced with good intentions,
delivered as regard.

"In God's name," they said.
And that settles it.

Rooms grew quiet
in ways prayer never does.

God's name was spoken,
but His nature went missing.

Questions loomed but stayed safely inside,
taught to sound like doubt,
and doubt to sound like sin.

Not because God said it.
But because power did.

You were taught this is love.
In God's name.

That His name could be swung
like a sanction,
that obedience meant full submersion
and no conversation.

"Whatever you do,
do it all in the name"
had a different beat to you
because you felt it
at the hands of one
supposed to be His own.

Gifts pushed and placed
on the altar for gain,
callings handled like leverage,
lifted for display.
In God's name.

Scripture bent mid-sentence,
meaning trimmed to fit the moment,
text rehearsed, mask on,
until it learned how to perform.

That proverbial throne they sat on
had them trippin',
doing verbal flips and
lyrical acrobatics,
timely theatrics
to keep folks subject to them.
In God's name.

But God's name
was never meant to be a gavel.

It was not given
to end conversations,
to shrink souls,
to baptize control
or excuse harm.

God does not need manipulation
to be obeyed.
Truth does not require fear
to be conveyed.

Intimidation is not a prerequisite
for power.
Shame is not a shortcut
for gain.

The name of the Lord
is a strong tower.
The righteous run to it
and are safe.

When language of faith is used
to force loyalty,
to deny dignity,
to quiet discernment,
it stops being guidance
and becomes something else.

If it leaves you smaller,
ashamed,
loath to speak honestly,
with God to blame,
or feeling like prey,
it may be many things.

But it is not God.

How in God's name?
How in God's name
can that be love?

Bully

Their own tears on the playground taught 'em:
words are stones
that can pack more punch
than a fist.
Thrown fast,
aimed sharp,
laughed off,
and forgotten.

Years later,
like uninvited guests,
the residue crests
and follows them home:
sneers and jeers trail them,
trouble hits,
their labels stick.

And they remember.

The Audacity of Freedom

Moses' Song

I used to wonder
how cries for freedom
became, in their ears,
insults,
threats,
and declarations of war.

How liberty sounded like violence
to the ones who thought they held the keys.

Until I encountered
chains of my own.

You've Met Her Before

Her dress was too short,
her lashes too long,
her outlook too dark,
her past all wrong.

She smelled like weed,
was too tatted up,
too loud, too much,
still not enough.

"Thou shalt not this."
"Thou shalt not that."
She fumbled, she cursed,
kept circling back.

She learned early
that "holy" eyes
could cut deep like a knife;
skewed vision and poisoned words
rewrote God in her mind.

She thought He frowned
when she stumbled off beat.
Thought He turned away
when she moved too free.

Thought her life was a test failed,
again and again.
Thought His love was diminished
by the weight of her sin.

But God didn't say that.
He doesn't keep score.
Doesn't count every fault,
then raise it once more.

No ledger, no tally,
no tightening noose.
No public conviction
for private wounds.

That voice was not Heaven.
It was heavy with pride,
a god made smaller
to fit them inside.

Mercy with an edge,
truth worn razor-thin.
A kingdom of cliques
for who's out and who's in.

Sadly, she carried it
like gospel verbatim,
like it came from God's mouth
instead of from them.

She wore their verdict,
like a scarlet letter on her chest,
until she learned
God speaks for Himself.

They said they knew God,
she believed that they did.
But the more she listened,
the further she slid.

God didn't say that.
That's not what He does.
They claimed His name,
but that wasn't Love.

God doesn’t need
a witness like that.
She felt too far gone
‘til God loved her back.

You’ve met her before.

Some still come carrying oil,
while others just carry shame.

Different clothes, different name.
Different past,
but the stigma’s the same.

She sits in the back
where the wary reside.
She’s learned when
to lower her eyes.

She’s what happens
when judgment drowns out grace.
Calls itself holy,
but leaves despair in its wake.

She's not rare.
You've seen her before.
Maybe this isn’t her story.
Maybe it’s yours.

Empty (2014)

(Originally written for the stage play "The Least of These")

For Freeman

I was empty like my cup.
"Fill me up," I'd say,
to anyone willing to listen or pay.

I must look a sight,
'cause they barely drop in pennies,
dissin' me left and right.

Is the price of love and kindness too high?
Is there anyone who cares,
anyone who dares to help me?

Can't understand how I found myself
on these streets with nothing left...
empty like my cup.

But… how did I get here?

This ain't the life I imagined for me.
Sure didn't see
this one coming…

Coming and going is all I do,
just trying to find food,
a little warmth and shelter each night,
just till morning light,
and time to do it all over again.

Time and time again I ask myself,
How did I get here on these streets
with nothing left?

Somebody, anybody, please help,
and then maybe I can free myself.

I'm not a bum, not a loser.
I didn't choose to be here.
I'm a human being going through,
just like you.

But I have lost big,
lost the life I once knew.
Lost myself,
my dignity too.

Fighting to survive the dirty looks
and crushing words.
Always being judged,
but never heard.

I'm on empty.
Don't want your sympathy.
Just a little respect,
a little less neglect.

A little love
goes a long way...

What You Answer To

They called you things
that weren't yours to carry.

Names spoken once,
then repeated
until they stuck,
like burrs in fabric,
like stains you stop trying to wash out.

Too much.
Nothing.
Problem.
Weak.
Loser.
Failure.
Dumb.
Freak.

And the other names too,
the ones they wouldn't say in a eulogy,
the ones that made you flinch,
the ones that essentially
changed how people saw you
or how you saw yourself.

A name can bless, bruise, crown you
or convince you to shrink.

Just think.

We name our children
before they can talk…
or choose, or even know who they are.

We name others carelessly,
as if labels don't stay,
as if the tongue leaves no trace.

And sometimes we name ourselves
out of pain, memory,
survival or mistaken identity.

But there is a difference
between a name you're given
and a name you believe,
between what they called you
and who you're called to be.

So lay the false names down,
what was never meant for you.
It's not what you hear,
it's what you answer to.

The truest name
is the one spoken by Love,
the one that restores sight,
not distorts it.

Say what's true,
what Love calls you.
Say it until you believe it,
until you finally see it.

Those other names
were never yours.

Imprint

You thought it would fade.

It was just a sentence,
just a glance,
just a mood,
just a moment among many.

But as they grow, you see it
in the way they hesitate
before answering you.

In the way they smile
to soften your opinion.

In the way they search your face
for signs of warmth.

In the words they choose,
the silences they keep,
the fear of judgment
still echoing in their steps.

In the moments they hold back,
or aren't themselves,
conforming instead
around the memory of you.

You don't remember what you said.
But they remember the feeling your words left behind.

Still Unlearning

We spoke harsh words we shouldn't,
threw stones we didn't mean.
Now we speak life, lift, nourish,
replace the shade with what is clean.

When words they hurl cause us distress,
our guard down, hearts exposed,
we speak truth, let God's word rest,
where shadows once imposed.

We own our words, the harm they've made,
and offer grace when sharp words fly.
We choose forgiveness, love displayed,
and speak with care as time goes by.

Still unlearning, day by day,
and letting love have final say.

SECTION IV.
THE WORDS THAT HEAL

Forgiveness, grace, and words that restore.

Your Voice Matters

Being silent when truth needs a sound.
Standing still when love needs to be loud.
Lifting your voice for the weary and worn.
Speaking hope into places bleak and forlorn.

What side are you standing on?

A whisper can pray.
A shout can awaken.
Let loose the fountain.
Your voice can move mountains.

Love Lifted Me

Sticks and stones may break bones.
But words, oh, how they wound.
Yet the same way words can bring decay,
words can also help improve.

They can be a tool for life
or else a tool for death.
But when nothing else can help,
Love will pull you through.

Remember to love
when breath is faint,
for love can be a lifeline.
Remember to love
the sinner, the saint,
for love is sure divine.

If you've ever slipped
to deepest depths
and somehow found your feet,
thinking back,
your heart will say,
Love lifted me.

Resurrection

O steady blessed Love,
how many times you entered souls
we thought were lost
and proved us wrong.

How often have you crossed
through the ash of ruined places,
lifting one small flame
we already named dead.

The Grudge (2013)

(Originally written for the stage play "Lessons in Love")

When was the last time someone hurt you
or stepped on your toes...
maybe betrayed you,
or left you alone...
broke your heart and protected their own?

When was the last time you cried
from the depths of your soul...
or fought back tears,
but could no longer hold
them back?

Back when you wore your heart
on your sleeve,
when showing your vulnerabilities
came easy...

Tears that flowed
because you've been broken,
heartaches and pains that perhaps
have never been spoken.

Think about that one person or persons,
those perpetrators of pain,
those who left a stain
on your heart...

With that thought in mind,
and in the passage of time
between that moment and now...
have you forgiven them?

Or does your conscience feel a little nudge
that maybe you've been holding a grudge
all this time?

I Forgive You

Offense was the chord that played
each time I tried to say them.
I cut my eyes,
I sighed and sighed,
while trying to obey Him.

I typed the words, recorded notes,
but had no nerve to send them.
And every cry and reason why
rose up then to upend them.

Though sincere pleas on bended knee,
petitions made with feeling,
my prayers went up like puffs of smoke,
bouncing off concrete ceilings.

When moments came that I fell short
and needed mercy new,
I remembered, God won't pardon me
'til I forgave them too.

Though time had passed
and still no words,
I started with a prayer,
hoping I would gain the strength
to extend forgiveness there.

But truth be told,
it came in waves;
emotions were the tide.
I had to give it all to Him
before flesh would subside.

"I forgive you" were the words I spoke,
but wasn't sure I'd ever mean them.
Said it fast, thinking it would last,
but I cringed when I would see them.

God understood just what I felt,
because He'd been there too.
"Father, please forgive them,
they know not what they do."

Familiar words, He'd said Himself
to those who'd done Him wrong.
If one deserved to hold a grudge,
surely it was God.

All the ways we reject Him
after giving us His life.
All the ways we disrespect Him
with pride, neglect, and strife.

We deny Him with our silence,
then blame Him for our pain.
We abandon what He died for,
yet still call out His name.

He was bruised by those He healed,
denied by trusted friends,
mocked by mouths He gave breath to,
yet loved them to the end.

If He could speak forgiveness,
while hanging from that tree,
then surely He could teach my heart
what grace must be in me.

So I practice saying "I forgive,"
to the air, to Him alone,
in letters never sent or read,
in mirrors, over groans.

And maybe one day face to face,
the words will finally stay.
But if or then, I choose love first,
and let God lead the way.

Say It Again, Slower

Say it again,
slower this time.
Be softer, gentler, kind.

Leave room
between the words,
for what broke
to breathe
and be heard.

Apologies don’t settle
when they rush.
They need pauses,
time, to trust.

Say it again, slower.
Be love's muse.
Like you’re learning
a language
once misused.

Learning a Softer Language

noun: softer language
words chosen to heal, not harm;
a gentle touch, a careful charm;
weighed in tone, intent, and calm.

verb: to soften
pause before you speak,
catch the words before they leave,
act as if peace is what you seek.

adjective: tender
prone to lift, repair, renew;
showing a kinder point of view;
becoming a pleasant, sweeter you.

usage:
Tender speech, repeat, refine.
Soften, listen first, align.
A *softer language* grows with time.

Honey

Some people are like honey:
slow pour, golden, naturally sweet.
They stick around,
warm, magnetic,
the kind of presence
that draws you in deep.

Breaking bread feels easy.
Time with them never feels spread thin.
Nothing forced and nothing rushed.
They pour patience
like sunlight coming in.

Their words soothe without deceit.
Their kindness wears no disguise.
Like honey settles, they listen,
waiting for invitation,
never prying.

Where vinegar stings,
honey coats like a balm.
It always leaves a trace:
peace as a signpost,
warmth like an ember,
trust as solid ground,
sweetness you remember.

The Church Alive

The church is more than walls or rows of pews,
more than sermons, lights, or Sunday songs;
and if you've only known its cracks and feuds,
you may have wondered where it all went wrong.

It lives wherever grace and mercy meet,
and gathers those who think they don't fit in.
It's like listening ears, hands that bring relief,
and praying for the lost and struggling.

Its strength is not in buildings standing tall,
but hearts made soft enough to bear another;
for Christ is seen not only in a call,
but in the ways we learn to love each other.

May we ever be a place where love is real,
the living body of the Christ revealed.

The Right Mix (2017)

(A weaving of stories revealing how purpose unfolds in divine timing)

Where I looked, I did not see.
Where I searched, there was no key.
Just a void, places lacking meaning,
that just wasn't me.

There were moments of pure ecstasy:
winning fights and claiming rights,
moonlit nights with friends and loved ones,
carefree days in the sun.

From the outside, I was living:
building, winning, rising.
But what you couldn't see
was something quite surprising.

See, what I had cooking
was the plan I thought was mine.
But God's recipe was
different ingredients, different timing.

There was more being prepared,
more than I had understood.
God was blending in the background
mixtures that I never would.

And though I moved in my own rhythm,
He never rushed the final taste.
And one day I found my purpose
wasn't wasted, nor misplaced.

Sanctuary

You were expected

Here is a place.
It waits.

Sit.
Breathe.
Rest if you need.

No one asks why you came.
No one shuns your name.

Your voice belongs.
No lefts, rights, or wrongs
close this door.

Every story, every scar, every step
has led to here.
Have no fear,
there is room.

Love Has Always Been Our Power

Before history wrote our story,
love was already here.

It lived in songs
rising from weary fields,
carried on the wind
to every listening ear.

In fathers speaking
and mothers singing
courage over children,
strong and sincere.

In quiet prayers
spoken before dawn,
asking faith to stay
and fear to disappear.

It walked hidden roads
toward freedom,
and sometimes back again,
shining light for others
through the dark.

It turned struggle into art,
music and poetry,
dreaming aloud of a world
where dignity wouldn't need a fight.

It sat firmly on buses
and stood unafraid in marches,
testifying boldly
that freedom is our right.

Generations planted hope
they might never see bloom:
prayers, sweat and tears
over long days and nights.

And still the harvest came.
Still hope stayed alive.

Through every season
hate has tried to divide,
love has held the line.

In every era meant to shake us,
and every chain meant to break us,
love is the tie that binds.

Love survived
in family,
in faith,
in community,
in open hearts.

We are living proof.

And long before history
recognized our strength
or honored this truth,

love
was already
our power.

What Grace Sounds Like

Before the cross, before the nails,
before the weight of blame,
Christ walked among the bruised and lost
and called them still by name.

His words were rain on dry hearts
and sick bodies; health sprang forth.
And when in life tempests did rage,
He spoke peace to their storm.

On the hill, the world held its breath,
as He awaited death's decree.
Betrayed by friends, denied by fear,
still mercy was His plea.

"Father, please forgive them,"
He prayed on their behalf.
Humbly bending to God's will,
not vengefulness or wrath.

And still that grace rings, strong and sweet,
flows from the cross to you and me.
Though hammer fell to place Him there,
it served to set us free.

Love held the weight He chose to bear,
and holds us still today, with care.

When the World Stood Still

(The Pandemic, 2019–2022)

When the world stood still,
we learned what we were made of.

Breath became precious,
air became suspect.
Status offered no shelter,
risk showed no respect.
And still, courage rose.

As hospitals overflowed,
as hands went unheld,
and final goodbyes
were spoken through glass,
essential hands showed up every day,
risking their lives like love always has.

Many stayed home for love's sake,
while life online became commonplace.

When isolation and grief
tried to set in,
neighbors checked in,
families bonded or reached across screens,
and strangers extended kindness,
voices uniting and reminding us
we were not alone.

Public spaces and churches went dark,
but prayer did not.

It traveled through phones,
through screens,
through homes
where living rooms became altars,
through writings of hope,

light sources, hushed voices,
and late-night tears.

Masks covered our mouths, but not our hearts;
we learned to read eyes,
to smile undercover
and realized it still translated,
to show compassion without touch,
to keep our distance
yet stay connected enough.

When some asked where God was,
He was there:
in endurance,
in mercy,
in courage,
in sacrifice,
in the daily choosing of love.

Millions of lives
were lost worldwide.
But billions survived.

With the same breath we feared losing,
we spoke life,
encouragement,
wisdom,
humor,
and light.

And words that were
spoken, typed, and sung,
love given, said and done,
when the world stood still,
helped heal what fear tried to claim.

Job's Song

Midnight of the Soul

I buried what I could not keep
and kept what I could not bury.
The night of my life grew heavy
with questions no answer could carry.

Still, hope reached for me in the darkness.
God spoke to me at long last,
in piercing starkness
that silenced
every question that I had.

And beneath the ash of great testing,
I found something unexpected:
newness, overflow, strength,
a life resurrected.

Reclaimed Words

Come back.
All of you.

The words I threw
when I was scared.
The ones I spat
when anger flared.
The ones I honed
to keep control.
The vows I spoke
before I grasped their toll.

Come back.

The verbal gut punches
when not loving me,
The senseless statements
of disbelief.
The negative words
I let remain,
The idle comments
with no restraint.

But language can be reclaimed,
surely redeemed.

Come back.

I will not rush you this time.
I will leave space
between the lines,
between your syllables
for breath,
for truth to act,
for grace to arrive intact.

You are not meant to wound.
You were never meant to hurry.
You were always meant
to carry weight,
and still fall gently.

Like fields restored after fire,
words can relearn their work:
how to bless,
how to heal,
how to cover,
how to still,
how to shape,
how to fill,
how to multiply
and till.

I ask them to mean
what they say,
and say what can be lived,
live what has been given,
what can be given away.

These are not new words.
They are words reclaimed,
words returned to purpose,
and in love, retrained.

I will speak you now again,
intentionally and aware,
as if love is listening
because love is there.

Stones or Seeds

To the head held low,
your smile is sunlight.
Your kindness,
morning dew on tired grass.

To the one lying awake at night,
your words for their pain
open a window.
Suddenly, they can breathe.

To the one starving for connection,
your steady "hello" and "how are you?"
are like a seat pulled closer.
Now, the silence isn't so loud.

To the one whose voice was ignored,
your "I hear you" raises the ceiling.
In that moment, the room feels larger.

To the child searching for language,
your patience becomes a bridge.
Your listening gives their heart wings,
teaching them they matter.

To the one unsure of themselves,
your affirmations and genuine praise
are a mirror held up gently
to show them you see them,
really see them.

To the one exhausted from trying,
your encouragement
is a bench along the road,
a welcome place to rest.

To the one on their sickbed,
your presence is fresh air.
Your prayers,
flowers where machines hum.

To the one afraid,
whose heart beats loud in their ears,
who's scanning for exits,
your calm voice becomes a cover.
Fear loses its grip.

To the one standing on the edge,
whose mind is racing fast,
your urgent words
become hands pulling them back.
Suddenly, their world stops spinning.

To the one in the thick of the fight,
your voice is a rallying cry,
strong enough to remind them
why they're still standing.

To the one wandering without direction,
your story becomes a trail of light,
just enough glow
to take the next step.

To the one who feels boxed in,
your faith becomes a blueprint.
Now, they see doors
where they were taught to accept walls.

To the one whose world
has lost its vibrant color,
your words are a spark.
Suddenly, the page listens.
The melody returns.

The brush finds motion.
The world exhales again.

To the one needing a chance,
you saying their name
ushers them into rooms
they've perhaps never seen
or couldn't reach.
And for the first time,
the room knows who they are.

Words can steady or shatter,
open doors or seal them shut.
They can cradle life
or bury hope.
Leave us speechless
with wonder, calm, or despair.

But when they sound like God,
they create newness,
transform chaos,
and call forth light.

So choose them carefully.
Because words don't just pass through the air.

Every word
is a stone or a seed.
You may forget which you threw,
but the ground remembers.

What the Wind Brings Back

The room was still,
but something in me moved.

Like dust in sunlight,
old grief rose,
then vanished.

It only settled somewhere
I could not see,
until the next time
the winds stirred.

Next time,
I will speak to the winds
and command my day differently.

The Seed

Even though dropped and buried
in a dark place,
drenched and nearly drowned
in what you thought
was a watery grave,

the sun was still shining
down on you,
calling forth life,
and you never knew...

Now, bloom.

Celeb-rated

Some lives are built beneath applause…

They know your name
when the lights are on you,
when the room applauds,
and you give 'til you feel used.

You learn to stand in it well,
to smile through it,
to give them what they came for.

You learn to be
the gift, the talent, the best.
And for a while, it feels
like love has a sound like clapping.

But what happens when the room grows quiet?
When no one's watching
and you're doing your thing in private?

You are still you
when the stage is gone.
Still you, when the praise falls off,
like costumes at the end of a show.

You are not the awards you hold,
not the work you complete,
not the titles you collect like proof that you matter.

They turn celebration into evaluation,
as if God's gift were something to be graded,
'til you're one celeb tired of being rated.

Listen, you are more than what you can do.
More than what you have done.
More than what they say
when you walk into a room.

You are a human *being*,
not a human *doing*.

And even before any name they give you,
you are always loved, always known,
without needing to perform.

So love what you do,
just not for applause.
And know that your true worth
comes from God.

Gatekeeper

Some words knock
like they belong:
accusations dressed as truth.
Old names.
Familiar threats.
Fear.

Not welcome here.

Not every thought
deserves a chair.
Not every voice
gets a say.

What condemns,
what diminishes,
just cannot stay.

What steals breath
and chokes sentences,
stops at the gate.

These are imaginations
cast down,
measured against truth
and found wanting.

This ground is kept
by what gives life.
By words spoken with grace.
By a Word far stronger
than words meant to debase.

What enters now
is refined,
has a distinct sound:
it must agree with love,
must carry light,
must echo truth,
must bow to the Divine.

God's voice
gives life to the hearer,
is the keeper,
the threshold,
the filter.
He is the gate,
incline your ear.
Everything else
is not welcome here.

SECTION V.
THE WORDS GOD SPEAKS

A voice that guides, calls, and sustains.

Before You Spoke

Before You spoke,
there was nothing.
Darkness covered the face of the deep.
Silence stretched wide
across a waiting void.

No edges.
No names.
No beginning yet brave enough
to call itself light.

Then You spoke,
and nothingness became
order, beauty and life.

And still,
before You speak into us,
there is that same ache of waiting,
the hush before meaning,
the stillness before direction.

We stand in the quiet,
unable to voice what we feel,
only knowing something within us
is waiting to be filled,
waiting to be called forth.

Before You speak,
our souls remember
what the world felt like
before the first dawn.

Speak, God.
Speak.

I'm Here

Creation keeps speaking
even when you don't listen.

Light.
Wind.
Trees bowing.
Clouds shifting.
Rain falling.
Eagle soaring.
Ocean waving.

Morning returning.

No words,
yet nothing is silent.

The world still knows
Who holds it.

I Asked God a Question

After I had prayed,
He answered me with a dream
that said, you're okay.
Woke with a blanket of peace
I could not explain away.

Rainbow On My Door (2009)

Nestled in the olive folds of fabric,
carried off in timeless deep thought,
the comfort of this spot seemed steady,
but in the throes of worry, I was caught.

Yet sitting at just the right angle,
like God intended for that brief spell,
as my daydream dissipated,
a sun ray wandered in and fell.

And made a rainbow on my door…

A burst of color in the shape of
a blank, but open scroll.
This flashing kaleidoscope began to roll,
and intrigue me.

As the sun weaved
between the clouds outside,
lighting up the room in brilliant splendor…

What troubled me before,
I could no longer remember.

Called By Name

You did not shout into the masses.
You did not mistake me for the crowd.
You called me by name.

Not the one life handed me,
but the one You knew
before fear, sin or shame
rebranded me.

Before a word was on my tongue,
You knew what it would be.
Before I could find myself,
You had already searched me.

You said I was Yours
before I ever believed I belonged.

Before I could answer,
You claimed me.
Before I could run,
You came.

When You spoke my name,
it sounded like a song
only a loving Father could sing.

And for a moment,
I was the only child in the world,
beloved child of the King.

I was precious in Your sight.
Seen.
Known.
Wanted.
Blessed.

And I answered the only way I could:
simply, yes.

I am Yours.

My View (2011)

If you could only see My view,
looking down through space.
Through stellar, blinding lights,
how is it I can see *your* face?
you might wonder.

My view of you is panoramic glory,
transcending the elements
and span of time,
taking in the complete picture,
the whole story.

My perfect creation -
future, present and past.
My vision, My plans
for you so vast,
for only I know
the first from the last.

Agape threads spiral down through the clouds,
beckoning to you like a lifeline.
Catch hold of this love
in epic proportion.
See the love in My eyes,
heart of Mine.

Piercing deep past the hues
of the sky's canvas,
black and blue, and purple,
colors of the rainbow, full
of the dye
I spread with My words.

Who but I
could see you like this?

My eyes are ever clear,
searching out your heart
for all that concerns you,
charting the course of your life
and seeing you through its stages.

There are pages and pages
of love letters I've written to you,
carried across the billions of miles of air
on My wind-blown kisses.

This is... My view... of you,
and it's bright,
and beautiful.

I Hear Your Prayers

You prayed,
and I heard you.

I hear the cries of your heart,
your whispered fears, your silent tears.
I see your seeking.
I am here,
listening,
answering,
moving.

Sometimes I say yes
and doors swing wide.

Sometimes I say no
because love sees farther
than desire.

Sometimes I say not yet
because timing is a language
you still learn.

And sometimes I am silent,
taciturn,
not absent,
not ignoring,
but working beneath the surface,
where roots grow strong
before fruit is seen.

But trust Me.
I heard you.

In the Stillness

There are words He whispers
in the stillness…

as I awake from a dream,
my listening notebook at my side.

just before I start to stir,
while the house is still quiet.

when I stand against the shore,
beholding the sunrise.

when I open the Scriptures,
and they open my eyes.

when I close my eyes,
as the world around me
flashes violently
for my attention.

I breathe in.
He breathes out.

And for a moment,
noise and storms align
with a quiet that shouts:

Be still.
I am God.

Still Speaking

The text is ancient,
but the voice is not.

Ink has aged,
paper has yellowed,
yet the Word keeps falling
on new ears,
arriving right on time.

You are not trapped in margins,
buried in history,
nor muted by doubt.
You are still speaking.

You speak into locked rooms,
into stubborn hearts,
into lives convinced
they've heard it all.

You speak to the hurting,
the searching,
the weary and the lost.
Still calling what is dead to rise.
Still correcting what wandered off.

Still speaking truth to lies,
making it all make sense.
Still loving with the voice of "I AM"
that will never be past tense.

Listen (2021)

Them voices in your head
keep telling you things you dread to hear.
Things you fear,
things that can keep you
darn near paralyzed
if you believe them lies.
Then you start to realize
that ain't God you're hearing.
That ain't love.

See, love sounds more like...
waterfalls rushing over your head:
"You are beautiful."
"You are strong."
"You have what it takes."
Because God don't make no mistakes.

Who's got you believing all that
"You ain't this" and "you ain't that"?
"Your good ain't ish,
It's just what they good at"?
It ain't no competition.
God's intention for you
is that you carry out *your* mission
that *you're* intended to do.

That mentality will be your fatality.
Staring and glaring, putting up a fight
to keep up with the Joneses.
But who's comparing, right?
Please don't let that be you.

Mirror, mirror on the wall
Who's the greatest of 'em all?
Listen...
Just be better than yesterday's view.
Better, stronger, wiser...
Catch *that* reflection, Boo.

You ain't wrong for loving yourself,
loving those who probably couldn't care less,
living your life as a light in a dark world.

Girl, listen...
Ain't nothing missing from you.
Everything sent to make you
devalue you ain't true.
What someone else can't see
ain't got nothing to do
with who you truly are.
Some folks are blind
and think they can see.
But if they could,
they would know
that everything God created,
He called good.

Man, listen...
All that sneak dissing,
them put-downs and snakes hissing,
intent on convincing you
that you ain't *shhhh…*
don't listen.
Unless it's constructive and uplifting.
Them bad intentions,
and I'm wishing – no, praying –
that you hear God instead.

He calls you His beloved,
So love yourself, king.
Diamond diva, you're royalty, queen.
And ain't no-thing anyone can do about it.

So ignore them lies
and heed what's true.
Hear the God in you.
Listen...

Honey From The Rock

I will feed you
where you thought nothing could grow.

From the rock, sweetness.
From the desert, provision.
From the struggle, strength.

Joy will bloom where sorrow lingered.
Light will shine where darkness grew.

I will sustain you.
Look to Me.
I am still good.
Taste and see.

Heaven's Vocabulary

Heaven does not waste words.

Its language is vast,
wide as oceans without a horizon,
deep enough to swallow our past.

Heaven calls light into being,
and darkness retreats without contest.

It speaks forgiveness,
and shame forgets its own name.

It declares peace,
and storms surrender their power.

And oh, the wonders Heaven knows:
wisdom beyond measure,
understanding past finding out.

Its King is omniscient,
the Source of all knowing,
the Author of truth itself,
nothing artificial in His intelligence.

Heaven's vocabulary
does not merely defy reality;
it decides it.

Every word carries weight.
Every syllable shifts atmospheres.
Every utterance creates what it commands.

When the King speaks a word, it succumbs.
What Heaven calls a thing, it becomes.

Your Times Are In My Hands

Do not dwell on the years behind,
do not count them lost.
I am the orchestrator of time,
I'm not bound by calendars or clocks.

I stand above it, outside it,
and I redeem it too.
Redemption was My mission
when I stepped into time for you.

Your seasons are not missed,
your moments are not a waste.
I use it all, converging for your good
at My own pace.

I am the Author of your days,
they stand at My command.
The days you have not yet seen
are already written in My hand.

In My hands is surely now,
and time is what I make it.
I am God, yesterday, today, forever,
no mistaking.

Your purpose is not expired,
your calling still remains.
So take your place,
stay in the race,
your now is yours to claim.

Return to Me

Leave the path that led astray,
turn your heart, come home today.
Come to Me, there's mercy here,
love enough to silence fear.

I am gracious, strong to save,
swift to cleanse what sin enslaved.
Though your stains were scarlet red,
I've called you justified instead.

I gave My Son,
He gave His life,
that you would walk forgiven, free.
So nothing now and nothing ever
separates your soul from Me.

The Word Became Flesh

He did not remain distant language.
He did not stay eternal sound.

He spoke Himself down
into time,
into a womb,
into the fragile house of flesh.

The Word drew breath,
felt the pang of hunger,
the sting of thirst,
immersed Himself
into humanity.

Divinity learned to walk.
Holiness learned to mourn.
Love, no longer abstract,
dwelled among us,
and could be touched.
Touched with the feeling
of our infirmities.

His mission was to many,
yet He still made time for one.
And we experienced Heaven
in one heart,
heard the Almighty
through one voice.

He made the choice:
His life for ours
the perfect sacrifice,
redeemed us once and for all,
then rose so we can rise.

And even now,
the Word remains…
not an echo or memory
that wanes,
but a living presence.

Effervescently speaking
and calling into being.
Still with us, and for us.
Still close enough
to know us
and touch us
with His love.

It Is Written (Abridged)

In arrant wilderness, as hunger crept in,
the tempter came smooth with a crooked grin,
but Truth stood firm and answered him:
"It is written."

When chaos covered the face of the deep,
no light, no form, no breath, no beat,
God spoke once, and life took shape:
"Let there be," and darkness gave way.
"It is written."

What pits and prisons tried to do,
what man meant for evil, God made good.
He rewrites stories like only He could.
"It is written."

When chains have held for years untold,
He speaks... and tyrants fold,
captives go, and seas unfold.
Bondage forever cannot hold.
"It is written."

When battles come and the odds say hide,
faith in God will turn the tide.
The sun once stilled at one man's cry.
"It is written."

From hidden fields to royal throne,
He calls the low and makes them known.
"It is written."

When giants roar and armies shake,
one voice of faith is all it takes:
"The battle is the Lord's."
Faith held its ground,
and the giant of pride came tumbling down.
"It is written."

When sickness speaks and fear takes hold,
"By His stripes..." you are healed and whole.
"It is written."

When wombs were closed and hope felt late,
He speaks, and new life will not wait.
"Sing, O barren…" lift your voice,
for empty places still rejoice.
"It is written."

When storms arise and winds contend,
at God's command, all raging ends:
"Peace. Be still."
Nature obeys,
and all the dark clouds roll away.
"It is written."

When demons shake and chains won't break,
one Word from Christ is all it takes:
"Come out."
In the name of Jesus, evil fades.
"It is written."

When weakness lingered, bleeding too much,
a woman reached in faith for just one touch,
and virtue flowed, it was enough.
Her faith brought healing.
"It is written."

When sin had left its crimson stain,
and none could break its binding chain,
He spoke a word: "It is finished."
And death lost its final sentence.
"It is written."

When death declares that all is sealed,
at His Word, graves must yield:
"Lazarus, come forth."
With Jesus, life can be restored.
"It is written."

When verdicts fall like judgment's fist,
the Word rewrites what courts insist:
"No condemnation."
Case dismissed.
Grace persists.
"It is written."

When love is twisted, cheap, unclear,
when fear disguises itself sincere,
the Word defines what love is here:
Patient. Kind. Enduring long.
Not self-seeking. Not led wrong.
"It is written."

When thoughts run wild and lies arise,
the Word cuts through deception's guise,
bringing every captive thought in line.
"It is written."

When identity is shed and blurred,
the Word restores what truth conferred:
"Chosen…royal…," not what they said,
but what God declared instead.
"It is written."

When history ends and time is done,
one Word remains, the faithful One.
Every knee will surely bow.
In glory then, or choose it now.
"It is written."

Say it in battle.
Say it in peace.
Say it till every lie has ceased.
It's what God said,
not what you feel.
The Word of God is final.
Sealed.
"It is written."

GOD IS LOVE

God does not borrow love
Or learn it from another source.
Divinity defines it.

It is not something He does,
Sometimes or selectively.

Love is His nature,
Origin and motive,
Voice and intention,
Every word shaped by it.

GOD IS LOVE.

SECTION VI.
AFTERLIGHT

Wisdom that lingers, softly glowing, and shared with love.

Fireflies

The pessimist kept them in a jar
long enough to kill the silly thought:
Light has wings, even encaged.

It was easier to believe in nothing,
to gather hopeless thoughts to themselves,
to think that darkness was a comfort,
and that miracles written in old books
and spoken in wooden pews
were false.

The optimist watched their tiny dances,
tiny sparks in thinning air,
knowing that faith
is patience enough
to see the glow survive
in spite of doubt.

The miracle of light
humming in small cages
reminded them that
faith's glow doesn't go out,
even in dark places,
and gentle, nail-scarred hands
will always open the lid
to let it fly.

They That Wait

Eagle's Grace

O eagle,
you who often fly alone,
yet never forsaken,
never in lack,
never in rivalry,
embraced by the heavens.

The eagle's eyes
were made for far horizons,
for what is coming
long before it arrives.

While other birds
braced on branches,
the eagle nested
where fear seldom follows,
watching for the moment
when the wind stirred.

The sky darkened.
Wind bent trees like signals.
But the eagle did not panic.
It waited,
then leaned into the wind
and rose,
on a current of grace.

From above the clouds,
rain lost its reach,
thunder softened into the distance,
and what once threatened
became background.

Some below called it reckless.
Others, foolish.
But the eagle understood its strength.

Those who learn this
do not live crouched down,
nor measure themselves against another.
They rise with patience
and confidence.

They understand that vision matters,
that altitude matters,
that waiting matters.

And that storms are not always sent
to break you;
sometimes they are sent
to carry you higher.

They Shall Not Want

Sparrow's Grace

They are stout and small,
not made for altitude,
they do not command the sky
nor traverse storms as some do.

Yet though they've faced their share of winds
and weather passing by,
their song and vision stay clear still,
unshaken as they fly.

They live close to the ground,
life's daily rhythms near,
among the seeking, never starved,
never ruled by fear.

They gather what is set within
the borders of their reach.
The morning brings them what they need,
the night finds them in peace.

Faithful for life...
They live and move within close care
where mercy does sustain,
with every flutter noticed,
every moment held the same.

But you pace the night
the sparrow rests through.
You fear tomorrow's weight.
Because your heart is restless,
and you do not trust today.

You measure worth by size and strength,
by how far you ascend,
by how the world applauds your flight
and rates your significance.

But provision asks for nothing more
than trust that will remain.
No grandeur buys what care provides,
no striving earns that claim.

So take heart...
If hands that shaped the heavens
will pause for sparrows small,
how much more will those same hands
not fail you should you fall?

And know this truth:
your value stands
beyond what your eyes can see.
You are worth far more than you imagine,
far more than one of these.

Peace from Sunrise to Sonrise

Dove's Grace

"The tender mercy of our God,
whereby the sunrise shall visit us from on high,
to give light to those who sit in darkness…
to guide our feet into the way of peace."
(Gospel of Luke 1:78–79)

The sun rises,
and a dove crosses the sky,
light gathering beneath its wings
as it passes by,
morning breaking open
as if giving birth
to the quiet promise
of peace on earth.

When the earth drowned
and the rain would not subside,
the dove set out over endless waters
looking for a mercy sign,
proof that judgment ceased.
It returned with hope in its mouth,
a single olive leaf.

As the Son rose from Jordan's stream,
heaven opened, what a sight,
and the Spirit made its descent
like a dove alights.

And all beheld…
God's presence made visible,
like purity with wings,
holiness drawing close,
renewing everything.

Ever since,
this gentle bird
shines the blessing of that moment:
that power can be quiet and still be heard,
that presence speaks with few words,
that peace unfolds in its time;
the dove is heaven's sign.

So each sunrise when doves take flight,
they echo the greater rising,
a promise made complete:
the Son Who came in mercy
and left us with His peace.

Song in the Night

The Word's Grace

Night stretches long
when the heart can't rest,
thick with thoughts that won't settle
and questions that refuse sleep,
a restlessness no sound seems to ease.

You search for relief in familiar places:
a swallow or a pill,
music playing softly,
voices passing time,
screens filling space,
anything to quiet the ache inside.

Yet every escape fails,
every song ends,
and the weight returns unchanged.

So you turn, at last,
to the pages long unopened
and begin to drink it in,
reading slowly,
holy words falling where they may.

Then a verse lifts from the page
as if it had been waiting
for your eyes only,
creating an opening of light
where shadow cannot stand.

Promises once memorized
rise from hidden places,
spoken again within you,
and begin to fill the hollow spaces.

Peace pours through like warm oil,
reaching crevices nothing else could touch,
calming every tension
with His words of love.

The room is consumed,
as you commune,
now filled with presence instead of heaviness,
as if heaven itself has drawn near
to carry you into the morning.

And you understand,
this is the song given in darkness,
a balm for whatever ails you,
God's voice illuminating your night,
the Living Word seeing you through.

The Sermon of Morning

The dawn arrives without a single word,
Yet something holy wakes in field and tree;
No choir is seen, yet praise is plainly heard,
Where light moves softly over land and sea.

The rivers preach by going where they must,
The mountains keep long silence without shame,
The seed breaks open in obedient trust,
And stars burn on with no desire for fame.

What book could hold the wisdom of the rain,
Or teach the patience written into trees?
Creation speaks again and yet again
To hearts too loud to hear such things as these.

If I grow still enough to understand,
I hear Your lovingkindness through the land.

Sermon of Submission

The Ocean's Grace

The ocean never strains to preach,
yet wisdom gathers at its shore;
its waves come back though pulled away,
obedient evermore.

It does not fear its depths unseen,
no eye can fully trace;
it bows itself before the moon
with calm and yielding grace.

The ocean speaks in repetition:
return, return, return;
each wave a small act of surrender,
each tide a lesson learned.

It cleanses what the land releases,
receives what storms and hearts disperse;
then sings in rhythms through the night
that hums in peaceful verse.

And standing where its vastness breathes,
the soul grows quiet, small…
for all creation seems to know
the voice behind it all.

And maybe that is reverence:
to move when God says move,
to carry peace within your depths,
and let your actions prove.

The Pages of You (2023)

If I flipped through the pages of your story,
where would my fingers land,
and linger...

Where would I feel you most,
know you deepest,
see you truest?

What does your life say
beyond the words on the page?

What Remains

In the end,
what remains of us
will not be our titles
or the rooms we filled.

It will be the sentences
others remember.

The promises we kept.
The mercy we offered.
The truth we dared to say.

Those words will travel
farther than we ever will...

Across generations,
across distant lands and skies,
and genomes,
known and unknown.

So let the last words we leave
be worthy
of the life we lived.

Candlelight

Could a simple breath
extinguish your fire?

All at once, on a birthday cake,
the years, counted and lit,
are blown away.
Still, life goes on.

How dare one careless exhale
from a single soul
be enough to douse your flame?

The years, like a struck match,
are enough to start a wildfire,
if you used just one.

How dare the embers stoked
from many nights by the fire
be put out by one blowing hot air?

Even the smallest flame
outlives the gusts
when tended,
when sheltered,
when mindful of what comes near.

The fire in you
is not yours alone,
but a spark meant to light
other candles along the way.

Could a simple breath
extinguish your fire?

No.
It only teaches you
how fiercely
you were meant to burn.

Inseparable

Neither height beyond the heavens,
nor depth beneath the seas,
nor time’s vast sweep,
nor death’s dark reach
can undo the bond
sealed in Christ’s love.
Held now, held forever.
Nothing can ever
separate me from God's love.

Say less.

Mean more.

Live it.

Scripture Echoes

The following passages helped shape the spirit of this collection.
They are not quoted so much as listened to.

Genesis 1
Genesis 8
Genesis 9:12-17
Genesis 50:20
Exodus 14
Joshua 10:13-14
1 Samuel 16-17
Isaiah 1:16-19
Isaiah 40:31
Isaiah 43:1
Isaiah 46:10
Isaiah 53:5
Isaiah 54:1
Isaiah 55
Isaiah 66:9
Jeremiah 1:5
Psalm 16:11
Psalm 19
Psalm 24
Psalm 42
Psalm 90:2,4
Psalm 139
Psalm 141:2
Proverbs 18:21
Joel 2:25
Zephaniah 3:17
Matthew 4–7

Mark 4:39
Mark 5
Luke 1:78-79
Luke 3:22
Luke 6:45
Luke 7:37-50
Luke 12:6-7
Luke 23:34
John 1:1–14
John 11
John 14:27
Romans 8:1; 28-39
1 Corinthians 2:16
1 Corinthians 13
2 Corinthians 10:5
Philippians 2:10-11
Colossian 3:12-16
Colossians 4:6
1 Timothy 2:5
Hebrews 7:25
Hebrews 12:29
Hebrews 13:8
James 3:5-10
1 Peter 2:9
Revelation 1:5-8
Revelation 2:4-5
Revelation 5:8

More From The Author

AVAILABLE NOW

Love Check: How Do You Measure Up?

COMING SOON

Afterlight (Short Story Collection)

Game of Hearts • Walking With Cane • and more
Stories of love, loss, hope, and revelation.

Love Check-In

Companion Workbook to *Love Check: How Do You Measure Up?*

SUBSCRIBE TO MY WEBSITE FOR UPDATES ON NEW RELEASES
www.MelanieDTheAuthor.com

OR SCAN THE QR CODE BELOW TO FOLLOW ME ON AMAZON

♥ Please Share Your Thoughts ♥

If this collection resonated with you,
I'd be grateful if you left a review on Amazon.
Reviews help others discover the book and support my work.

Feel free to also share favorite poems or how a poem connected with your story. Your words may be the encouragement someone else needs.

PLEASE SCAN THE QR CODE BELOW:

www.ingramcontent.com/pod-product-compliance
Lightning Source LLC
LaVergne TN
LVHW012332100826
845148LV00017B/2115

* 9 7 9 8 2 3 4 0 5 3 7 5 6 *